The Official

RANGERS
Annual 2015

Written by Andrew Dickson

Designed by Duncan Cook

© 2014. Published by Grange Communications Ltd., Edinburgh, under licence from Rangers Football Club. Printed in the EU.

Main photography by Kirk O'Rourke and © The Rangers Football Club Limited. Additional images from Willie Vass and Press Association Images. Unless otherwise indicated all trademarks are the property of The Rangers Football Club Limited.

ISBN: 978-1-908925-72-5

A Grange Publication

£7.99

Club Honours

European Cup Winners' Cup (1):
Winners 1972, Runners-up 1961, 1967

UEFA Cup:
Runners-up 2008

Scottish League Champions (54):
1891, 1899, 1900, 1901, 1902, 1911, 1912,
1913, 1918, 1920, 1921, 1923, 1924, 1925,
1927, 1928, 1929, 1930, 1931, 1933, 1934,
1935, 1937, 1939, 1947, 1949, 1950, 1953,
1956, 1957, 1959, 1961, 1963, 1964, 1975,
1976, 1978, 1987, 1989, 1990, 1991, 1992,
1993, 1994, 1995, 1996, 1997, 1999, 2000,
2003, 2005, 2009, 2010, 2011

SPFL League One Champions (1):
2014

SFL Division 3 Champions (1):
2013

Scottish Cup Winners (33):
1894, 1897, 1898, 1903, 1928, 1930, 1932,
1934, 1935, 1936, 1948, 1949, 1950, 1953,
1960, 1962, 1963, 1964, 1966, 1973, 1976,
1978, 1979, 1981, 1992, 1993, 1996, 1999,
2000, 2002, 2003, 2008, 2009

Scottish League Cup Winners (27):
1946/47, 1948/49, 1960/61, 1961/62,
1963/64, 1964/65, 1970/71, 1975/76,
1977/78, 1978/79, 1981/82, 1983/84,
1984/85, 1986/87, 1987/88, 1988/89,
1990/91, 1992/93, 1993/94, 1996/97,
1998/99, 2001/02, 2002/03, 2004/05,
2007/08, 2009/10, 2010/11

Contents

6 Simply the Best

8 Season Review

18 Champions Again Ole Ole!

20 Goals of the Season

22 Sandy Jardine: A Legend Lost

24 Stats and Appearances

26 There's No Place Like Home

28 Player Profiles

38 Ibrox Arrivals

40 Born in the USA!

42 Youth Review

48 A Centre of Excellence

50 Lee McCulloch's Dream Team

52 Quiz

53 Wordsearch

54 Eat Like a Player

56 The Treble Winners

58 Remember When?

60 Quiz Answers

61 They Said It!

62 Where's Broxi?

Simply The Best

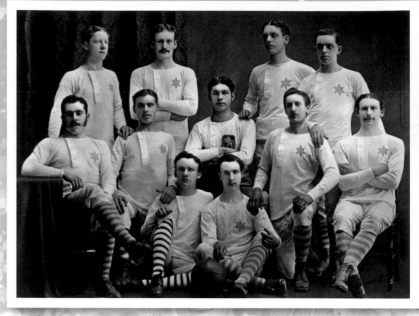

One of the first Rangers teams which included two of the club's Founding Fathers, Peter Campbell (back row, second right) and Moses McNeil (middle row, far right)

Rangers are the most successful football club in Scotland, having won the national championship a world record 54 times in total.

Yet despite claiming so many trophies in their 142-year history, the Light Blues came from very humble beginnings in 1872.

Back then, they were founded by four teenage boys whose simple wish was to form a team that played the emerging sport of association football.

Little did brothers Moses and Peter McNeil, William McBeath and Peter Campbell know at that point what a huge sporting institution their creation would go on to become.

The quartet came together in Glasgow's West End Park — known now as Kelvingrove Park — and started a side which played it first game against Callander and drew 0-0.

That game took place at Fleshers' Haugh on Glasgow Green and the venue was the first of a few homes for Gers in their nomadic early years.

After also playing at Burnbank and Kinning Park, they moved to the original Ibrox Park before settling on their current site in 1899.

By then the team had won its first outright title having shared the inaugural Scottish League with Dumbarton in 1891.

Three Scottish Cups had been claimed too by that point as

Rangers started to establish themselves as one of the country's leading teams.

The 1910s and 20s saw many more crowns claimed as William Wilton then Bill Struth took charge as the team's first two official managers.
Under Struth in particular, great strides were made and he oversaw 30 major honour wins to cement his status as the club's most profitable boss to date.

He finally left in 1954 after a remarkable 34 years at the helm and his replacement, Scot Symon, continued in the same vein as he followed up with six championships.

Symon also took the side to the last four of the European Cup in 1960 before reaching the 1961 and 1967 European Cup Winners' Cup finals, losing each time.

There would be continental success for Rangers, however, in 1972 as they won at the deciding stage of the latter

The Trophy Room at Ibrox Stadium

competition for the first time at the third attempt. Dynamo Moscow were beaten 3-2 in Barcelona and the triumph was poignant in many ways as the club's finest hour came less than 17 months after its darkest.

The Ibrox Disaster on January 2, 1971 resulted in the death of 66 Light Blues supporters when there was a crush on a stairway following a derby with Celtic.

To this day, it remains one of the worst tragedies in British football history and those who passed on will never be forgotten.

The late 1970s saw Rangers become the dominant force in Scotland again after Celtic had dictated for so long and under Jock Wallace, they claimed trebles in 1976 and 1978.

Walter Smith and his assistant Archie Knox enjoyed huge success together in the 1990s

match Celtic's feat of the 1960s and 70s.

During that spell, Smith almost took Gers to the final of the first Champions League and saw his side just miss out to eventual winners Marseille.

Dick Advocaat and Alex McLeish both enjoyed success in respective spells in the hot seat before Paul Le Guen's brief, unhappy reign led to Smith's return for a second tenure.

Once more he drove the team on and it reached the 2008 UEFA Cup final against Zenit in Manchester but fell at the last hurdle as it lost 2-0.

Nevertheless, there were other triumphs and by the time Ally McCoist took over from Smith

in 2011, the legendary manager had 21 honours to his credit.

McCoist's first steps as his own man were difficult as the club encountered financial difficulties and ultimately administration in 2012.

But he has overseen a strong recovery on the pitch as both the Third Division and League One titles have been secured by huge point margins.

Rangers still have work to do before they can come close to reliving some of their glories of the past.

But they're undoubtedly on the rise again and having reacted positively to adversity in the past, they are doing that once more.

Graeme Souness

There was to be another downturn but the arrival of Graeme Souness as player/ manager in 1986 changed that.

He laid the foundations from which Walter Smith later built upon and between them, they claimed nine titles in a row between 1989 and 1997 to

Moving on Up

Having won the Third Division by a handsome 24-point margin in their first ever season outside the top flight of Scottish football, Rangers' task in 2013/14 was to continue their upward rise through the ranks back to the Premiership where they belong.

Winning promotion was a must, ideally with overall victory in the revamped League One, and it was to be a campaign of considerable improvement as they achieved both objectives in style. Here's the story of how they won a place in the current Championship competition.

< Chris Hegarty celebrates scoring against Brechin

July/August

After an excellent pre-season which saw Rangers enjoy successful warm-up fixtures in Northern Scotland, England, Germany and Holland, they began their year in style with a solid 4-0 win over Albion Rovers in the Ramsdens Cup.

For the first few weeks of the new campaign, the Light Blues were hindered by the fact they weren't yet allowed to register the players who had agreed to sign for them in the summer.

That meant some of the recent arrivals were only allowed to play in certain matches as trialists, with those coming in from clubs outwith Scotland not allowed to play at all until September. Despite those restrictions, Gers adapted well and showed signs of what they could do as they cruised past Rovers into round two, with new recruit Nicky Law scoring an impressive double.

There was a strong start to League One too, with Ally McCoist's men topping the table from the third minute of their 4-1 win over Brechin thanks to Chris Hegarty's opener.

A 3-0 success at Stranraer was relatively trouble-free while a 6-0 rout of Airdrie was the outcome at the end of a terrific performance at New Broomfield.

August was rounded off with a 5-0 thrashing of East Fife at Ibrox as skipper Lee McCulloch scored his first career hat-trick four days after Berwick were beaten in the Ramsdens Cup.

That provided a much better end to the month than the start had been, which had seen Rangers fall at the first hurdle in the League Cup with a surprise 2-1 extra-time loss at Forfar.

Moment of the Month

The style of play in the victory at Airdrie had fans oozing with excitement as the hard graft of pre-season paid off with a slick performance in Lanarkshire.

Striker Jon Daly said: "To score six goals away from home is obviously tricky to do but it was great for me to get my first two for the club that night.

"It was a great game for all of us who were involved. It was a strange situation to have some players prevented from playing and I'd never encountered that before.

"Despite that, we were still able to do well overall in the first few weeks. The manager wanted us to lay down a marker and I think we did that."

July/August Fixtures

28/07	Ramsdens Cup, R1 4-0 at Albion Rovers (Law 2, Black, Templeton)
03/08	League Cup, R1 1-2 AET at Forfar Athletic (Aird)
10/08	League One 4-1 v Brechin City (Hegarty, Law, Black, Shiels)
17/08	League One 3-0 at Stranraer (Little, Macleod, McCulloch)
23/08	League One 6-0 at Airdrieonians (Macleod, Little, Crawford, Daly 2, Law)
27/08	Ramsdens Cup, R2 2-0 v Berwick Rangers (McKay, Little)
31/08	League One 5-0 v East Fife (Clark, McCulloch 3, Macleod)

< Jon Daly grabs his second at Airdrie

September

As September arrived, Rangers' year-long transfer embargo came to an end and that meant they were free to use all nine of their new summer signings without restriction.

Jon Daly and Nicky Law had played most often up to that point and they had enjoyed good starts to their Ibrox careers.

But Cammy Bell and Nicky Clark had made just

Jon Daly enjoys his four-goal salvo against Stenny

one appearance each while Stevie Smith, Richard Foster, Bilel Mohsni, Steve Simonsen and Arnold Peralta hadn't played at all.

Seven of the imports started the opening match of the month against Arbroath and it seemed nerves got the better of them as it was goalless at half-time then they fell behind.

Gers came back well, however, and a debut goal from Mohsni; a second consecutive Lee McCulloch hat-trick, and an Andy Little strike ensured a 5-1 success.

There were three more games before the month was out and each of them brought a win, starting with a 3-0 victory at Queen of the South.

That took Gers into the last four and it was a sweet moment for them after they had lost to the Doonhamers in the quarter-finals of the previous year's event.

A 1-0 win at Forfar was scrappy as Little struck again but it did at least go some way towards making up for the League Cup setback there a few weeks earlier.

The home clash with Stenhousemuir six days later was at the opposite end of the scale and the Light Blues racked up what would be their biggest victory of the season.

Their 8-0 scoreline could easily have run into double figures as Daly scored at Ibrox for the first time then went on to get three more goals.

Moment

Beating Stenny kept the good feeling at Rangers going strong as the team kept up its 100 per cent record in the league and began to pull clear of their rivals.

Forward Andy Little said: "From the very start of that game, I was getting in on goal quite a few times and their defence played a very high line.

"That just played into our hands and especially at Ibrox, where we've usually got quite a lot of the ball.

"We did well and we hoped that would be a sign of things to come. We did start the season very well and September was good for us."

September Fixtures

14/09	League One 5-1 v Arbroath (Mohsni, McCulloch 3, Little)
17/09	Ramsdens Cup, QF 3-0 at Queen of the South (Mohsni, Daly, McCulloch)
22/09	League One 1-0 at Forfar Athletic (Little)
28/09	League One 8-0 v Stenhousemuir (Daly 4, Little, Wallace, Templeton, Mohsni)

Andy Little was the matchwinner at Forfar

October

October was a month of away fixtures for Rangers and they won them all but it was far from easy, despite the chain of results allowing them to take a tighter grip of the League One lead.

A 2-0 success at Ayr United was comfortable but it took until the second half before Bilel Mohsni and Lewis Macleod's goals edged the visitors in front.

Bilel Mohsni laps up his opener at Ayr

It was a similar story nearly three weeks later at East Fife, where it was once again goalless at the break then Gers pressed home to a 4-0 victory thanks to Jon Daly's hat-trick.

At the end of the month, it took until 16 minutes from the end for Daly to strike and help the Light Blues into the Ramsdens Cup final at Stenhousemuir's expense by a single goal.

Indeed, Ally McCoist's side scored 11 times in October and all bar one of those strikes came after the interval.

The one which arrived before then came in a quite remarkable game at Brechin City, where Rangers came so close to losing.

In terrible rain, they fell 2-0 behind after just 10 minutes and although Daly pulled one back, the Glebe Park team restored their cushion as they moved 3-1 in front.

It would require something special in the second period to turn things around and Nicky Clark's introduction as a substitute made a huge difference.

Mohsni made it 3-2 before Nicky Law's shot from a wide area sneaked in at the back post to pull his team level.

Brechin nearly won the contest moments from the end but they hit the bar and just seconds later, Clark nodded in David Templeton's cross to seal a sensational comeback.

Moment of the Month

Rangers weren't at their best against Brechin but there's no doubt the spirit and desire they showed to come from behind and win was impressive.

Midfielder Nicky Law said: "What happened at Brechin was new to us and a lot of it was our own doing. We were sloppy and gave away goals we wouldn't normally give away.

"We got a rollicking from the manager at half-time and we had got a reminder of how tough the league is.

"He got everyone going and from there we showed great character at a difficult venue to come back and win 4-3."

October Fixtures

06/10	League One	2-0 at Ayr United (Mohsni, Macleod)
19/10	League One	4-3 at Brechin City (Daly, Mohsni, Law, Clark)
26/10	League One	4-0 at East Fife (Thom OG, Daly 3)
29/10	Ramsdens Cup, SF	1-0 at Stenhousemuir (Daly)

<Nicky Clark's late winner at Brechin was crucial

November

There were only three League One fixtures in November as the month started and finished with Scottish Cup matches.

In the first, Airdrieonians came to Glasgow under former Ibrox defender Gary Bollan and were beaten 3-0 as Jon Daly scored twice and David Templeton also found the net.

Jon Daly was a regular scorer in November as he found the net in seven successive games

That set up a tough trip to Championship side Falkirk in round four and the Light Blues showed their class once more to win, with Nicky Law and Templeton making the difference.

In the title race, Gers were yet to drop a point and a trio of victories kept them on track to claim the trophy early and gain a second promotion in a row.

Dunfermline travelled from Fife and proved to be one of the toughest opposition sides of the season as their physical approach left Rangers rattled.

Andy Little broke his jaw and cheekbone; Bilel Mohsni broke his nose; Lee McCulloch needed stitches in a head wound, and Richard Foster suffered a serious ankle injury.

But Ally McCoist's men overcame all of those problems to seal a 3-1 success, with McCulloch's penalty setting them on their way before Daly and Mohsni struck.

Airdrie came back to Govan on league business but were dealt the same fate as Daly and McCulloch – again from the spot – condemned them to a 2-0 reverse.

Elsewhere, Arbroath were beaten 3-0 on a crisp night on the North Sea coastline and Daly was on the mark for the seventh game in succession at Gayfield.

Moment

It was a different sort of fixture to the win at Brechin the previous month but Rangers had to show more resolve as they beat Dunfermline despite mounting injury problems.

Midfielder Ian Black said: "It was a tough game and Dunfermline were probably the most physical side we came up against all season.

"We got to know that quickly because tackles were flying in and boys were getting injured everywhere.

"Despite that, it was important we stuck to our game plan and matched up with them. We played well on the night and thoroughly deserved our win."

November Fixtures

01/11	Scottish Cup, R3 3-0 v Airdrieonians (Daly 2, Templeton)
06/11	League One 3-1 v Dunfermline Athletic (McCulloch pen, Daly, Mohsni)
09/11	League One 2-0 v Airdrieonians (Daly, McCulloch pen)
25/11	League One 3-0 at Arbroath (Daly, Donaldson OG, Clark)
30/11	Scottish Cup, R4 2-0 at Falkirk (Law, Templeton)

<Lee McCulloch's penalty broke the deadlock against Dunfermline

December

Christmas is a time for giving but not necessarily on the football park, yet it was on Boxing Day Rangers finally gave up their perfect League One record as they drew 1-1 with Stranraer.

Before then, results had remained good and Nicky Clark had a night to remember at the start of December as he scored four times in a

Nicky Clark tapped in on the line to score against Dunfermline

6-1 win against Forfar.
Adding to the occasion was the fact the attacker's quadruple – his first for the club – came on his mum Liz's birthday.

The following weekend, a 3-0 win was recorded at home to Ayr but then there was a 19-day

wait to play again as a trip to Stenhousemuir was postponed because of bad weather.

Having a pause in play did more harm than good as Gers were stale when they returned to action.

Taking on Stevie Aitken's Stranraer side, they sneaked in front through Lee McCulloch's penalty before the break but then found themselves hanging on in the closing stages.

And they paid the price for a rare lapse in concentration as Jamie Longworth equalised deep in injury time to record a famous result for the Blues.

The response to that result was strong and Rangers finished 2013 on a real high as they thrashed closest challengers Dunfermline 4-0 at East End Park.

Fraser Aird opened the scoring and second-half additions from Nicky Clark, Nicky Law and Robbie Crawford had fans smiling ahead of the bells for New Year.

Moment

Nicky Clark had been in and out of the team since arriving at Ibrox but he showed what

he is capable of with his deadly quartet against Forfar.

The former Queen of the South player said: "Scoring four goals for Rangers is a special feeling and to do it on my mum's birthday was nice as well.

"It was my first hat-trick for the club so I was delighted to do that at Ibrox in front of our fans and I went out to celebrate with my family afterwards.

"Drawing with Stranraer was disappointing and

we were under pressure to bounce back but we did that. Our performance at Dunfermline showed what fighting spirit we have."

December Fixtures

03/12 League One
       6-1 v Forfar Athletic
       (Clark 4, Wallace, McCulloch pen)

07/12 League One
       3-0 v Ayr United
       (Daly, Aird, Mohsni)

26/12 League One
       1-1 v Stranraer
       (McCulloch pen)

30/12 League One
       4-0 at Dunfermline Athletic
       (Aird, Clark, Law, Crawford)

January

It's fair to say 2014 didn't get off to the most spectacular of starts for Rangers, even if they won all five of their games in January.

With Scottish Cup and Ramsdens Cup ties still awaiting them further down the line, they remained focused on their League One campaign.

Lewis Macleod's goal was enough to beat Airdrie at New Broomfield

And although it wasn't always as exciting as it could have been, the Light Blues still got the job done as they began to build a run of victories once again.

They followed up their win at Dunfermline with a single-goal success at Airdrieonians, with Lewis Macleod getting it.

Nicky Law's double either side of half-time at Stenhousemuir brought a 2-0 victory there, while Dean Shiels got a brace of his own to secure the same result at home to East Fife.

Steven Simonsen made his debut at Forfar as Cammy Bell became a father for the first time and the Englishman produced one of the saves of the season in a 2-0 win at Forfar.

At the other end of the park, Bilel Mohsni's header and spectacular individual effort from David Templeton ensured away fans left Station Park happy.

Arbroath came to Ibrox hoping to spring a surprise and certainly did that as they twice went in front, including in the first minute of the game.

But Gers came back each time through Jon Daly and Templeton before a Lee McCulloch penalty swung the tie in the home side's favour.

Moment of the Month

Dean Shiels had had a terrible time trying to come back from a knee injury nine months after sustaining it and his double against East Fife was a pivotal moment for him personally.

The ex-Kilmarnock playmaker said: "It was great to be back playing and to score two goals in that game was brilliant.

"The boys had done ever so well to beat Airdrie and Stenhousemuir so it was nice to return to Ibrox and for me to find the net and win us the game.

"It maybe wasn't the most exciting month of the season but our results were solid and we deserved the wins we were getting."

January Fixtures

02/01 League One
1-0 at Airdrieonians (Macleod)

05/01 League One
2-0 at Stenhousemuir
(Law 2)

11/01 League One
2-0 v East Fife
(Shiels 2)

20/01 League One
2-0 at Forfar Athletic (Mohsni, Templeton)

25/01 League One
3-2 v Arbroath
(Daly, Templeton, McCulloch pen)

<Dean Shiels was at the double against East Fife

February

For only the second time in the season, Rangers dropped two points in February as they drew 3-3 at home to Stenhousemuir, a team they'd thrashed 8-0 on their last visit.

Park in a 2-0 win against Ayr United.

The draw with Stenny was a strange affair as the visitors went ahead twice, fell behind at last with just under 20 minutes left then battled back to get a draw.

A rare Lee Wallace goal set Rangers on their way to victory at Stranraer

Law and Daly scored either side of an own goal but the Warriors deserved credit for the improvement they had shown since their previous trip to Ibrox.

The month ended well with a 2-0 victory at Stranraer, with vice-captain Lee Wallace and Jon Daly on the mark.

Rangers kept advancing in the Scottish Cup as well

But otherwise it was a month of positives as more wins in League One came and the finishing line came into sight.

Dean Shiels and Jon Daly did just enough to make sure Brechin were beaten 2-1 and Nicky Law then Jon Daly scored at Somerset

and they did so with their best showing of the competition yet against Dunfermline.

In-form Shiels scored a treble while David Templeton, who was making a big impact after breaking back into the side, also got on the scoresheet in a 4-0 win.

Moment of the Month

David Templeton's direct style, allied with Dean Shiels' creativity, was adding a new dimension to Rangers' play and that was clear in the Scottish Cup win over Dunfermline.

The former Hearts winger said: "I felt we played really well in the first half. We took our chances and that gave us a comfortable lead going into half-time.

"Thankfully we came out in the second half and did the same sort of thing. We managed to get another good goal and we could have won by even more.

"The third goal was crucial as it killed them off. The biggest thing in the second half for us was to come out

and keep doing what we were doing in the first. We did well to do that."

February Fixtures

01/02	League One 2-1 v Brechin City (Shiels, Daly)
07/02	Scottish Cup, R5 4-0 v Dunfermline Athletic (Shiels 3, Templeton)
15/02	League One 2-0 at Ayr United (Law, Daly)
22/02	League One 3-3 v Stenhousemuir (Law, McMillan OG, Daly)
25/02	League One 2-0 at Stranraer (Wallace, Daly)

<David Templeton scores in the 4-0 Scottish Cup win over Dunfermline

March

With just four points dropped, Rangers claimed the League One title with eight games to spare as Airdrieonians were beaten 3-0 on March 12.

Lee McCulloch's penalty winner at East Fife had given the Light Blues the opportunity to clinch the title against the Diamonds and they were never going to let that chance slip.

Calum Gallagher capped his debut against Dunfermline with a goal

Having stumbled over the finishing line in 2013, they crossed it this time with conviction as McCulloch's third hat-trick of the season – including two spot kicks – sealed the victory.

That wasn't the only highlight that month though. A 2-0 win against Dunfermline three days later brought Stevie Smith his first goal in more than seven years with a wonderful free kick.

Youngster Calum Gallagher also made his debut as a substitute and grabbed the clincher in the closing stages.

He then set up Fraser Aird's opener in a Scottish Cup replay with Albion Rovers three days later at Hamilton's New Douglas Park.

The sides had drawn 1-1 initially, with Bilel Mohsni scoring a late leveller to force a rematch, but Gers would win at the second time of asking as Jon Daly made it 2-0.

Aird scored in three consecutive games and the other two were 2-1 wins against Brechin and Arbroath.

The Light Blues had gone to City having not lost an away goal in five months but that proud run came to an end as Nicky Clark got the winner in a narrow success.

Moment

Beating Airdrie to win the title meant Rangers claimed the prize almost as quickly as it was possible to at the start of the season as they did it having won all bar two of their games.

Fraser Aird said: "Getting the early goal pumped us up even more and gave us the lift required to go on and win the match and Lee scored a great hat-trick once again.

"It was a massive weight off our shoulders once we got over the finish line because we felt we had to keep going strongly.

"We had stumbled quite a bit on our way to the Third Division title and had a few draws but we were more consistent this time."

March Fixtures

01/03 League One
1-0 at East Fife
(McCulloch pen)

09/03 Scottish Cup, QF
1-1 v Albion Rovers
(Mohsni)

12/03 League One
3-0 v Airdrieonians
(McCulloch 3, 2 pens)

15/03 League One
2-0 v Dunfermline Athletic
(Smith, Gallagher)

18/03 Scottish Cup, QFR
2-0 at Albion Rovers
(Aird, Daly)

23/03 League One
2-1 at Brechin City
(Aird, Clark)

29/03 League One
2-1 at Arbroath
(Daly, Aird)

<Lee McCulloch and Ally

April

April brought Rangers their most disappointing spell of the season as they lost back-to-back games to drop out of two knockout tournaments.

Having gone 39 games unbeaten in all competitions, they were into the Ramsdens Cup

Games but there was no advantage gained as the Arabs won 3-1.

Gers had played much better in that second game and they took their improved form into the rest of the month as they notched a quartet of league wins.

Dean Shiels nets in convincing 4-0 win at Stenhousemuir

Ian Black scored what was later voted as the club's Goal of the Season in a 3-0 win over Forfar then Stenhousemuir were beaten 4-0 at Ochilview.

Rangers made hard work of their 2-1 victory against Ayr as Bilel Mohsni twice put his team in front either side of Alan Forrest's equaliser.

final as favourites but surprisingly lost 1-0 in extra-time to Raith Rovers in Edinburgh.

There was a chance to make up for that the following week as the Light Blues faced Dundee United in the last four of the Scottish Cup.

The game was played at Ibrox with Hampden Park being redeveloped for the Commonwealth

They were sharper as Stranraer came to Ibrox for the final match there of the campaign and the hosts didn't disappoint ahead of the League One trophy presentation.

Fraser Aird and Dean Shiels scored before Arnold Peralta's first competitive goal for the club rounded off a 3-0 victory.

Moment of the Month

Collecting the League One trophy at the end of a good home campaign in the competition was a moment for everyone to savour.

Captain Lee McCulloch said:

"It was a long wait for the trophy but when you're captaining Rangers and lifting silverware in front of a full house it doesn't get much better.

"We did well to be so consistent over the course of the season against a lot of part-time teams who had a very specific game plan which they didn't deviate from.

"That made it tough for us but we were still able to get the right results against sides which sat in and made it tough for us."

April Fixtures

06/04 Ramsdens Cup, F
       0-1 AET

12/04 Scottish Cup, SF
       1-3 v Dundee United
       (Smith)

15/04 League One
       3-0 v Forfar Athletic
       (Black, Mohsni, Shiels)

19/04 League One
       4-0 at Stenhousemuir
       (Smith, Shiels, McCulloch pen, Law)

22/04 League One
       2-1 v Ayr United
       (Mohsni 2)

26/04 League One
       3-0 v Stranraer
       (Aird, Shiels, Peralta)

May

With 35 games played, just one more remained in League One for Rangers going into May and with it came the chance to make history.

Not since the 1898/99 season had the Light Blues gone a whole league campaign without

Rangers' season ended with a 1-1 draw at closest rivals Dunfermline

losing a match and that was the only time that feat had been achieved in the club's history.

Back then, the team had won all 18 games as the title was claimed and while there wasn't a 100 per cent record any more this time, the players were keen to stay unbeaten.

Standing in the way of Ally McCoist's team was Dunfermline, the side which had been confirmed as the second-placed side behind the champions.

After a goalless first half, Dean Shiels broke the deadlock and it seemed victory might be achieved but in the end Gers had to settle for a 1-1 draw.

That was disappointing as it meant a perfect record away from home in the third tier had come to an unwanted end.

But defeat had been avoided, meaning the Ibrox outfit finished their schedule with 33 wins and three draws.

In turn, they had won the title by 39 points from the Pars and had clearly kicked on from the previous campaign.

A place in the 2014/15 Championship alongside the likes of Hearts, Hibernian and Falkirk awaited as life in the big time got a little closer again.

Moment of the Month

Drawing with Dunfermline brought the campaign to a low-key end but it did ensure Rangers became the first Light Blues side in 115 years to go through a whole league season unbeaten.

Manager Ally McCoist said: "We weren't great at Dunfermline but 33 victories out of 36 games and three draws? I think they're great figures.

"It's difficult to criticise our players. They continued to raise their level of performance and win games after they won the league very early in the season.

"A lot of people will say that should be the case and they're right but a bit of psychology does come into it and our lads kept going to remain undefeated."

<Gers players applaud fans at East End Park

May Fixture

03/05   League One
1-1 at Dunfermline Athletic
(Shiels)

Final Table

	P	W	D	L	F	A	PTS
Rangers	36	33	3	0	106	18	102
Dunfermline	36	19	6	11	68	54	63
Stranraer	36	14	9	13	57	57	51
Ayr United	36	14	7	15	65	66	49
Stenhousemuir	36	12	12	12	57	66	48
Airdrieonians	36	12	9	15	47	57	45
Forfar Athletic	36	12	7	17	55	62	43
Brechin City	36	12	6	18	57	71	42
East Fife	36	9	5	22	31	69	32
Arbroath	36	9	4	23	52	75	31

CHAMPIONS AGAIN

Goals of the Season

Rangers scored a magnificent total of 130 goals in their 48 competitive games during 2013/14, with Ian Black's strike against Forfar in April being named Goal of the Season.

Here's a look back at that excellent effort along with the other nine contenders which were nominated for the prize.

NICKY LAW v Airdrieonians
August 23, 2013

As Rangers thrashed Airdrie 6-0 with a great performance, Law scored an outstanding team goal as he flicked in following a wonderful passing move involving Lewis Macleod, Jon Daly and Andy Little.

LEE McCULLOCH v Arbroath
September 14, 2013

Having scored a hat-trick in his previous outing against East Fife, skipper McCulloch fired this 30-yard screamer into the top corner on his way to another hat-trick in a 5-1 victory after Arnold Peralta's free kick hit the wall.

LEWIS MACLEOD v Ayr United
October 6, 2013

Having scored a spectacular effort against East Fife in August, Macleod bettered it with a perfectly-executed overhead kick in a 2-0 success at Somerset Park after Peralta's corner was nodded back to him by Bilel Mohsni.

JON DALY v East Fife
October 26, 2013

Having already scored once in Methil, Daly's second of a hat-trick in a 4-0 win was an excellent header as he looped one over the goalkeeper after Peralta's cross had deflected and been flicked on by Nicky Clark.

NICKY CLARK v Forfar Athletic
December 3, 2013

Clark would go on to score four goals in a 6-1 victory against Forfar. His first was a fine rising header from 12 yards which soared into the top corner from a Lee Wallace cross.

JON DALY v Ayr United
December 7, 2013

This was a simple but ruthlessly-finished goal from striker Daly as he leapt highest to send a flying header in at the near post from a well-delivered Ian Black free kick in a 3-0 success.

DAVID TEMPLETON v Forfar Athletic
January 20, 2014

With Rangers ahead by just one goal in Angus, Templeton made it two as he collected Macleod's pass, cut inside past three men and arrowed an unstoppable shot into the top corner from 15 yards.

DEAN SHIELS v Brechin City
February 1, 2014

Similar to another effort against Brechin back in August, this was a mirror image as Shiels curled

a lovely left-footed effort across the keeper and into the far top corner to open the scoring in a 2-1 win.

STEVIE SMITH v Dunfermline Athletic
March 15, 2014

Having scored the first goal of his career against Dunfermline, Smith's second came with the Pars providing the opposition too. This was an excellent curling left-footed free kick from nearly 30 yards in a 2-0 victory.

IAN BLACK v Forfar Athletic
April 15, 2014

With Rangers seeking a breakthrough against Forfar, it came in style as Black flicked the ball up with his right foot then hammered the opener into the top corner with his left from 35 yards to kick-start a 3-0 win.

SANDY JARDINE: A LEGEND LOST

There were few setbacks for Rangers on the park as they eased to the League One title but they suffered a massive loss off it when club legend Sandy Jardine passed away in April.

The campaign had begun with the iconic ex-defender unfurling the championship flag before the opening game against Brechin following the Third Division title win in 2012/13.

Sadly the final home match was preceded by Jardine's death two days earlier after a battle with cancer and he's somebody who is hugely missed by everyone connected with the club.

Seen by so many as everything a Ranger should be, the former full-back represented the club ever so well almost constantly for half a century.

Signed as a schoolboy at the age of 15, 'Sandy' was actually a nickname for a young man called William Pullar Jardine and it came about because of the colour of his hair.

He would travel from Edinburgh to Glasgow for training each day with John Greig and little did they know then they would become two of the most revered men in the Gers' history.

The young Jardine played a variety of positions in the team before making the right-back role his own and it was

there he developed into one of the world's best.

He helped the Light Blues win the European Cup Winners' Cup in Barcelona against Dynamo Moscow in 1972 having scored against Bayern Munich in the semi-finals.

He also won three championships in his time at Ibrox as well as five Scottish Cups and five League Cups.

Jardine was a key man in the Treble-winning squads of 1976 and 1978 and won the Scottish Football Writers' Player of the Year prize before both of those

successes in 1975.
He claimed the same accolade 11 years later while at Hearts, another club he served with distinction, and also won it as part of the Scotland team which played at the 1974 World Cup.

Jardine's international career saw him earn 38 caps in total and he scored once in a 2-0 win over Wales in 1974.

After he hung up his boots, he worked in a number of roles at Rangers on the

commercial side at the club including in public relations.

Jardine latterly served as a player liaison officer and after the club went into administration in 2012, he led protests against the SFA at sanctions imposed on Gers fans he felt were unfair.

He led around 10,000 supporters to Hampden Park to deliver a letter expressing

unhappiness at the actions taken and he defended the club to the very end.

When Jardine died, it was no surprise that tributes to him poured in from leading football figures around the world.

Rangers players, staff and fans expressed their grief too and many left scarves and strips at the Copland Road gates outside Ibrox as marks of respect.

With a wonderful man's passing, a legend had been lost and the likelihood is we'll never see anyone as remarkable as Sandy again.

	League	Scottish Cup	League Cup	Ramsdens	Total
Fraser **AIRD**	22 (5) 5	4 (2) 1	0 (1) 1	1 (2) 0	27 (10) 7
Cammy **BELL**	31 (0) 0	5 (0) 0	0 (0) 0	3 (0) 0	39 (0) 0
Ian **BLACK**	32 (0) 2	5 (0) 0	1 (0) 0	4 (0) 1	42 (0) 3
Nicky **CLARK**	13 (9) 9	2 (2) 0	0 (0) 0	1 (2) 0	16 (13) 9
Robbie **CRAWFORD**	6 (13) 2	0 (1) 0	1 (0) 0	3 (0) 0	10 (14) 2
Emílson **CRIBARI**	4 (3) 0	0 (0) 0	0 (0) 0	1 (0) 0	5 (3) 0
Jon **DALY**	34 (0) 20	6 (0) 3	0 (0) 0	4 (0) 2	44 (0) 25
Sébastien **FAURE**	22 (4) 0	2 (2) 0	1 (0) 0	2 (2) 0	27 (8) 0
Richard **FOSTER**	19 (4) 0	4 (0) 0	0 (0) 0	3 (0) 0	26 (4) 0
Scott **GALLACHER**	3 (0) 0	0 (0) 0	1 (0) 0	2 (0) 0	6 (0) 0
Calum **GALLAGHER**	1 (3) 1	1 (0) 0	0 (0) 0	0 (1) 0	2 (4) 1
Chris **HEGARTY**	1 (0) 1	0 (0) 0	1 (0) 0	0 (0) 0	2 (0) 1
Kyle **HUTTON**	2 (7) 0	2 (0) 0	0 (0) 0	1 (0) 0	5 (7) 0
Nicky **LAW**	32 (0) 9	6 (0) 1	0 (0) 0	4 (0) 2	42 (0) 12
Andy **LITTLE**	13 (8) 5	0 (3) 0	1 (0) 0	3 (1) 1	17 (12) 6
Lewis **MACLEOD**	16 (2) 5	2 (0) 0	1 (0) 0	3 (0) 0	22 (2) 5
Kyle **McAUSLAND**	3 (1) 0	0 (0) 0	0 (1) 0	1 (1) 0	4 (3) 0
Lee **McCULLOCH**	34 (0) 17	6 (0) 0	1 (0) 0	5 (0) 1	46 (0) 18
Barrie **McKAY**	0 (2) 0	0 (0) 0	0 (1) 0	0 (1) 1	0 (4) 1
Andy **MITCHELL**	0 (0) 0	0 (0) 0	1 (0) 0	0 (0) 0	1 (0) 0
Bilel **MOHSNI**	28 (0) 10	6 (0) 1	0 (0) 0	3 (0) 1	37 (0) 12
Andy **MURDOCH**	0 (2) 0	0 (0) 0	0 (0) 0	0 (0) 0	0 (2) 0
Arnold **PERALTA**	17 (3) 1	3 (0) 0	0 (0) 0	2 (0) 0	22 (4) 1
Dean **SHIELS**	13 (5) 8	3 (0) 3	0 (0) 0	1 (0) 0	17 (5) 11
Steve **SIMONSEN**	2 (0) 0	1 (0) 0	0 (0) 0	0 (0) 0	3 (0) 0
Stevie **SMITH**	11 (2) 2	1 (0) 1	0 (0) 0	2 (0) 0	14 (2) 3
Charlie **TELFER**	0 (1) 0	0 (0) 0	0 (0) 0	0 (0) 0	0 (1) 0
David **TEMPLETON**	9 (11) 3	2 (2) 3	1 (0) 0	1 (3) 1	13 (16) 7
Lee **WALLACE**	28 (0) 3	5 (0) 0	1 (0) 0	5 (0) 0	39 (0) 3

25

There's No Place Like Home

IBROX STADIUM has been home to Rangers for 115 years and it remains one of the most iconic and well-loved arenas in European football.

Nowadays it's a modern, all-seated stadium with a seating capacity of 50,987 but it has changed quite considerably over the decades.

Gers actually used a number of other locations as home grounds first before they settled into their current surroundings.

Their very first match took place at Fleshers' Haugh on Glasgow Green and they later resided at Burnbank in the city's west end and in Kinning Park. From there, the Light Blues moved to the Ibrox area for the first time some 15 years after their foundation but even then it wasn't to their current venue.

Instead, they played roughly 100 yards closer to Copland Road and it was only in 1899 they switched to where they remain today.

The first version of the ground was the scene of 25 deaths in 1902 when a section of wooden terracing collapsed at a Scotland-England match and that led to redevelopment.

Earth slopes were moulded around the pitch, thus creating a much bigger capacity, and the present-day Main Stand designed by renowned architect Archibald Leitch opened in 1929.

A decade later, a derby with Celtic attracted a new record crowd for a league fixture in Britain of 118,567 and that has never been beaten since.

There were further tragedies and in 1961, two fans died in a crush before 66 more perished in 1971 when Stairway 13 collapsed after

another game against Celtic. The latter incident in particular is one which still haunts Rangers fans and it was the catalyst for drastic alterations which reshaped Ibrox into what we inhabit now.

Willie Waddell, the club's manager, visited a number of grounds in West Germany and decided to model the modernised stadium on Borussia Dortmund's Westfalenstadion.

By 1981, the ground's old oval shape had gone and three new stands had been erected as part of a rectangular layout, with a new capacity of 44,000.

Only the Main Stand remained and in 1991 that had a third

tier called the Club Deck added to it to increase how many people could attend games.

Over the years, it hasn't just been Rangers matches Ibrox has hosted and indeed it hasn't just been football either. On top of cup semi-finals and finals and Scotland internationals, it was where the rugby sevens competition at the 2014 Commonwealth Games took place.

Ibrox has also been a venue for concerts by the likes of Bon Jovi, Frank Sinatra, Rod Stewart, Simple Minds and Elton John.

As time goes on, more and more new venues rise elsewhere which are clearly more advanced than Rangers' home.

Nevertheless, its age is outweighed by its character and the love fans have for it and its popularity is as high now as ever before.

FRASER **AIRD**

Position:	Midfielder
Date of Birth:	February 2, 1995
Nationality:	Canadian
Debut:	September 23, 2012
	v Montrose (H)
Previous Club:	None

An exciting winger who first broke into the side in the early part of the 2012/13 season, Aird has made himself an important first-team player in the time since. Having started 25 of the last 26 games last term and come on as a substitute in the other, he's someone manager Ally McCoist trusts and his direct approach and eye for goal make him a tricky opponent. Born and raised in Toronto, Canada, Aird has been capped for Scotland at youth level.

CAMMY **BELL**

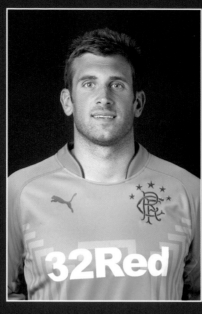

Position:	Goalkeeper
Date of Birth:	September 18, 1986
Nationality:	Scottish
Debut:	August 31, 2013
	v East Fife (H)
Previous Club:	Kilmarnock

A Scotland international who won his first cap in 2010 against Faroe Islands, Bell arrived at Ibrox in the summer of 2013 and quickly made himself the regular first-team goalkeeper. He impressed as he took over the position from previous number one Neil Alexander and kept 25 clean sheets in 39 appearances. Formerly of Kilmarnock, Bell won the League Cup with them in 2012 and hopes for more major honours during his time with the Light Blues.

IAN **BLACK**

Position:	Midfielder
Date of Birth:	March 14, 1985
Nationality:	Scottish
Debut:	July 29, 2012
	v Brechin City (A)
Previous Club:	Heart of Midlothian

Black is a combative midfielder whose tough tackling and gritty style has often made him a target for opponents in the past. Although he doesn't score many goals, the former Hearts player can strike the ball well from a distance and he scored the club's Goal of the Season in 2013/14 against Forfar. Capped for Scotland against Australia while playing in the Third Division with Rangers, Black has also turned out for Inverness and started out at Blackburn.

NICKY **CLARK** ROBBIE **CRAWFORD** JON **DALY**

	NICKY CLARK	ROBBIE CRAWFORD	JON DALY
Position	Forward	Midfielder	Forward
Date of Birth	June 3, 1991	March 19, 1993	January 8, 1983
Nationality	Scottish	Scottish	Irish
Debut	August 31, 2013	July 29, 2012	July 28, 2013
	v East Fife (H)	v Brechin City (A)	v Albion Rovers (A)
Previous Club	Queen of the South	None	Dundee United

Clark really came to prominence in the 2012/13 season when he scored a remarkable tally of 41 goals for Queen of the South and with his contract up there the following summer, Ally McCoist moved to bring him to Rangers. The striker scored nine goals in his first year at Ibrox but it was a disjointed campaign as he was sidelined for more than two months at one point with a broken foot. When he was fit, he showed he can make an excellent contribution.

An excellent athlete who was once a school cross country champion, Crawford is a talented midfielder who perhaps hasn't played as often as his ability suggests he could have done. Slick on the ball and someone who weighs in with occasional goals despite spending much of his time as a substitute, he is an able squad player and somebody who has every chance of making a bigger impact in times to come with the League One champions.

Signed after leaving Dundee United in 2013, Daly's first season at Ibrox saw him win the Sam English Bowl awarded to Rangers' leading league scorer as he netted 20 times in that competition and 25 overall. A player of great experience following several years in English football, the Irishman's support play is often as big an asset as his knack for breaching defences. Daly's biggest weapon is undoubtedly his head and he's a real threat at set-pieces.

DYLAN DYKES   SEBASTIEN FAURE   RICHARD FOSTER

	Dykes	Faure	Foster
Position	Midfielder	Defender	Defender
Date of Birth	March 14, 1996	January 3, 1991	July 31, 1985
Nationality	Scottish	French	Scottish
Debut	N/A	August 30, 2012	September 17, 2013
		v Falkirk (H)	v Queen of the South (A)
Previous Club	None	Olympique Lyonnais	Bristol City

A young midfielder who went into 2014/15 still looking for his first-team debut, he's a player who did a lot in the previous campaign to work his way into manager Ally McCoist's thoughts. Scoring nine times for Gordon Durie's academy side including a number of penalties, Dykes was a key performer as the side finished second in the inaugural SPFL Under-20 League and went on to win the SFA Youth Cup on penalties against Hearts after a 2-2 draw in Paisley.

Someone who can also operate as a holding midfielder, Faure's best positions are in defence where he plays either as a centre-half or a right-back. Previously contracted to Ligue 1 side Lyon, the youngster was part of the French team which finished fourth at the FIFA Under-20 World Cup in Columbia in 2011. Faure has shown considerable improvement in his two years so far at Rangers and manager Ally McCoist's likes his physical approach.

Now in his second spell at Ibrox, Foster returned to Rangers in the summer of 2013 from English side Bristol City after previously spending time on loan in Glasgow from Aberdeen during the 2010/11 season. Back then, the full-back helped Walter Smith's team win the SPL title and impressed in the Champions League against the likes of Manchester United and Valencia. A former winger, Foster turned out in that position for Scotland at under-21 level.

CALUM GALLAGHER   LUCA GASPAROTTO   CRAIG HALKETT

Position: Forward	**Position:** Defender	**Position:** Defender
Date of Birth: September 13, 1994	**Date of Birth:** March 3, 1995	**Date of Birth:** May 29, 1995
Nationality: Scottish	**Nationality:** Canadian	**Nationality:** Scottish
Debut: March 15, 2014	**Debut:** April 13, 2013	**Debut:** N/A
v Dunfermline Athletic (H)	v Clyde (H)	**Previous Club:** None
Previous Club: None	**Previous Club:** None	

A striker who can also perform on the right flank, Gallagher made an instant impact on his first-team debut against Dunfermline in March when he drew a foul from Danny Grainger which resulted in him being sent off before scoring the clincher in a 2-0 win. He followed that up with his first start two days later in a Scottish Cup replay against Albion Rovers and set up Fraser Aird's opener in another 2-0 win in the last eight of the competition.

Canadian centre-half Gasparotto first got a taste of competitive action with Rangers towards the end of the 2012/13 season when he debuted against Clyde and appeared in further games with Peterhead, East Stirlingshire and Berwick. The defender didn't appear at first-team level last term but was an integral part of the successful under-20 squad and also enjoyed a three-game loan spell with League Two outfit Stirling Albion in December and January.

Halkett was Luca Gasparotto's regular central defensive partner at under-20 level in 2013/14 as the pair developed a good understanding together. More versatile than his team-mate, the Scotland under-19 cap can also play at right-back and made a good impression as a striker for Gordon Durie's team when required last campaign having started his career in that position. Halkett was an unused substitute in a game at Ayr United in February.

KYLE HUTTON   LIAM KELLY   NICKY LAW

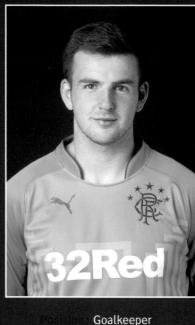

Position: Midfielder	**Position:** Goalkeeper	**Position:** Midfielder
Date of Birth: February 5, 1991	**Date of Birth:** January 23, 1995	**Date of Birth:** March 29, 1988
Nationality: Scottish	**Nationality:** Scottish	**Nationality:** English
Debut: August 14, 2010	**Debut:** N/A	**Debut:** July 28, 2013
v Kilmarnock (H)	**Previous Club:** None	v Albion Rovers (A)
Previous Club: None		**Previous Club:** Motherwell

One of Hutton's first tasks as a Ranger was to shackle Manchester United stars Paul Scholes and Ryan Giggs in the Champions League back in 2010 and he is a midfielder who can dictate games when he is at his best. He struggled with injuries last season as ankle ligament damage and a broken leg sidelined him for long spells but Hutton was given a new one-year contract and is determined to establish himself in the first XI once and for all.

Kelly is still very inexperienced but has plenty of potential and oozes confidence whenever he plays. The youngster is a promising Murray Park academy graduate who first came to prominence with a fine display during the penalties win over Celtic in the 2012 Glasgow Cup final and stood out again last season in an 8-7 shoot-out victory over Hearts in the SFA Youth Cup final. As well as saving four kicks, he also scored the winner himself.

A box-to-box midfielder with a welcome habit of finding the net, Law was Ally McCoist's first signing of the 2013 close season and the Englishman is now a key player in his side. He played in the English Premier League at the age of 17 with Sheffield United against Manchester United and once interested Tottenham Hotspur but the move never materialised. Law has since played for Yeovil Town, Bradford City, Rotherham United and Motherwell.

MACLEOD	McAUSLAND	McCULLOCH

Midfielder	Defender	Defender
June 16, 1994	January 19, 1993	May 14, 1978
Scottish	Scottish	Scottish
July 29, 2012	July 28, 2013	July 31, 2007
v Brechin City (A)	v Albion Rovers (A)	v Zeta (H)
None	None	Wigan Athletic

One of the brightest prospects to come from the Murray Park Youth Academy in recent years, Scotland under-21 cap Macleod is an exciting midfielder who has already scored a number of spectacular goals in the early part of his career. He missed the second half of each of the last two seasons through injury and illness but did enough before each lay-off to show what an important player he can be for the club for years to come.

A versatile defender who began his career as a striker, McAusland made his debut for Rangers at the start of last season against Albion Rovers in the Ramsdens Cup and turned in more decent displays against the likes of Airdrieonians and East Fife before going on loan to Ayr United for the rest of the season. Going to Somerset Park wasn't a new thing for the Cumnock youngster, who had spent much of the previous campaign there too,

Rangers' captain arrived at Ibrox in 2007 from Wigan and has experienced it all with the Light Blues, winning top-flight titles, Scottish Cups, League Cups and playing in a UEFA Cup final with the team he grew up supporting. Now playing mainly in defence, ex-Scotland star McCulloch can also play in midfield and up front and scored three hat-tricks against East Fife, Arbroath and Airdrieonians as League One was one with comfort last season.

BARRIE McKAY   BILEL MOHSNI   ANDY MURDOCH

	McKAY	MOHSNI	MURDOCH
Position	Midfielder	Defender	Midfielder
Date of Birth	December 30, 1994	July 21, 1987	January 30, 1995
Nationality	Scottish	Tunisian	Scottish
Debut	May 13, 2012	September 14, 2013	August 31, 2013
	v St Johnstone (A)	v Arbroath (H)	v East Fife (H)
Previous Club	None	Southend United	None

One of the most naturally talented ball players at Rangers, McKay spent the second half of 2013/14 away from Ibrox as he went on loan to Morton in the Championship. He first showed what he's capable of when he scored a sublime goal in a 2-0 friendly win at Linfield aged 17 and was a regular in the side as the Third Division was claimed in 2012/13. McKay started out at Kilmarnock but made his senior breakthrough with the Light Blues.

Now an international player after making his debut for Tunisia in the summer, Mohsni is one of the big characters in Ally McCoist's squad and he's as effective in attack as he is at the back, having scored 12 times last season. His tally of one goal per three games wasn't a huge surprise as he had played as a striker for his old club Southend and he once nearly joined English Premier League side West Ham but a trial there was unsuccessful.

What Murdoch lacks in height he makes up for in heart as he goes about his business with grit and steel in midfield. A youngster who is highly rated by the management at Rangers, he captained the under-20 team to its SFA Youth Cup final win against Hearts last season. The teenager made his first-team debut against East Fife last year and although he didn't feature much more; that should change as time goes on.

CALUM GALLAGHER

LUCA GASPAROTTO

CRAIG HALKETT

Position	Forward
Date of Birth	September 13, 1994
Nationality	Scottish
Debut	March 15, 2014
	v Dunfermline Athletic (H)
Previous Club	None

Position	Defender
Date of Birth	March 3, 1995
Nationality	Canadian
Debut	April 13, 2013
	v Clyde (H)
Previous Club	None

Position	Defender
Date of Birth	May 29, 1995
Nationality	Scottish
Debut	N/A
Previous Club	None

A striker who can also perform on the right flank, Gallagher made an instant impact on his first-team debut against Dunfermline in March when he drew a foul from Danny Grainger which resulted in him being sent off before scoring the clincher in a 2-0 win. He followed that up with his first start two days later in a Scottish Cup replay against Albion Rovers and set up Fraser Aird's opener in another 2-0 win in the last eight of the competition.

Canadian centre-half Gasparotto first got a taste of competitive action with Rangers towards the end of the 2012/13 season when he debuted against Clyde and appeared in further games with Peterhead, East Stirlingshire and Berwick. The defender didn't appear at first-team level last term but was an integral part of the successful under-20 squad and also enjoyed a three-game loan spell with League Two outfit Stirling Albion in December and January.

Halkett was Luca Gasparotto's regular central defensive partner at under-20 level in 2013/14 as the pair developed a good understanding together. More versatile than his team-mate, the Scotland under-19 cap can also play at right-back and made a good impression as a striker for Gordon Durie's team when required last campaign having started his career in that position. Halkett was an unused substitute in a game at Ayr United in February.

KYLE **HUTTON** LIAM **KELLY** NICKY **LAW**

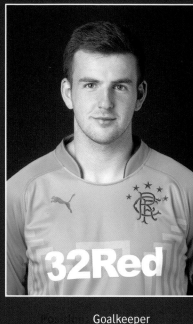

Position:	Midfielder
Date of Birth:	February 5, 1991
Nationality:	Scottish
Debut:	August 14, 2010
	v Kilmarnock (H)
Previous Club:	None

Position:	Goalkeeper
Date of Birth:	January 23, 1995
Nationality:	Scottish
Debut:	N/A
Previous Clubs:	None

Position:	Midfielder
Date of Birth:	March 29, 1988
Nationality:	English
Debut:	July 28, 2013
	v Albion Rovers (A)
Previous Club:	Motherwell

One of Hutton's first tasks as a Ranger was to shackle Manchester United stars Paul Scholes and Ryan Giggs in the Champions League back in 2010 and he is a midfielder who can dictate games when he is at his best. He struggled with injuries last season as ankle ligament damage and a broken leg sidelined him for long spells but Hutton was given a new one-year contract and is determined to establish himself in the first XI once and for all.

Kelly is still very inexperienced but has plenty of potential and oozes confidence whenever he plays. The youngster is a promising Murray Park academy graduate who first came to prominence with a fine display during the penalties win over Celtic in the 2012 Glasgow Cup final and stood out again last season in an 8-7 shoot-out victory over Hearts in the SFA Youth Cup final. As well as saving four kicks, he also scored the winner himself.

A box-to-box midfielder with a welcome habit of finding the net, Law was Ally McCoist's first signing of the 2013 close season and the Englishman is now a key player in his side. He played in the English Premier League at the age of 17 with Sheffield United against Manchester United and once interested Tottenham Hotspur but the move never materialised. Law has since played for Yeovil Town, Bradford City, Rotherham United and Motherwell.

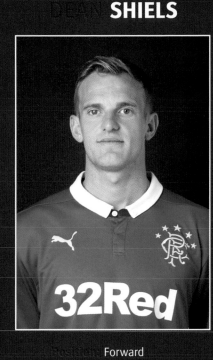

	PERALTA	SHIELS	Simonsen
Position	Midfielder	Forward	Goalkeeper
Date of Birth	March 29, 1989	February 1, 1985	April 3, 1979
Nationality	Honduran	Northern Irish	English
Debut	September 14, 2013	August 7, 2012	January 20, 2014
	v Arbroath (H)	v East Fife (H)	v Forfar Athletic (A)
Previous Club	Vida	Kilmarnock	Dundee

Honduras internationalist Peralta was hugely unlucky in the summer as a thigh injury picked up on the final day of the season at Dunfermline ruled him out of his country's squad for the World Cup finals in Brazil after he had initially been included in the 23-man pool. A feisty midfielder, the former Vida player had a mixed first season in Scotland but he finished it well with his first goal for Rangers in the final home match of the campaign against Stranraer.

Shiels took a while to get going in 2013/14 as he felt the after-effects of a medial ligament injury in his knee but he went on to score 11 times in all competitions including a Scottish Cup hat-trick against Dunfermline to show he's back to his best again. A creative player who adds so much to the team when he's on song, the Northern Ireland international started out at Arsenal and his since appeared for Hibernian, Doncaster Rovers and Kilmarnock.

Once signed for Everton by Walter Smith for £3.3million, Simonsen is an ex-England under-21 international who has English Premiership experience having turned out previously for Stoke City. He only played three times in 2013/14 because Cammy Bell's form was so good but on his debut against Forfar he produced a stunning one-handed reaction save to prevent a Lee Wallace own goal. It was one of the best stops in a Gers game all campaign.

RYAN SINNAMON

Position: Defender
Date of Birth: July 22, 1996
Nationality: Scottish
Debut: N/A
Previous Club: None

A composed right-back who can also play on the left, Scottish youth international Sinnamon is someone Ally McCoist is eager to ease into his side over the course of time. An SFA Youth Cup winner with the club in May 2014, the youngster appeared as an unused substitute the previous month for the first team at Stenhousemuir and it seems only a matter of time before he'll be getting such opportunities on a more regular basis.

STEVIE SMITH

Position: Defender
Date of Birth: April 30, 1985
Nationality: Scottish
Debut: September 14, 2013
v Arbroath (H)
Previous Club: Portland Timbers

Smith started his career at Rangers as a youth player but left in 2010 after a pelvic injury hindered his progress. Fully fit again and with his problems behind him, he returned to Ibrox in the summer of 2013 after spells with Norwich, Aberdeen, Preston and MLS side Portland Timbers. After scoring just once in his first stint with Gers, he grabbed three goals last term including two excellent free kicks against Dunfermline, Dundee United and Stenhousemuir.

DANNY STONEY

Position: Forward
Date of Birth: May 5, 1996
Nationality: Scottish
Debut: April 13, 2013
v Clyde (H)
Previous Club: None

One of the more confident players at Rangers, teenage striker Stoney is someone with undoubted potential who can fulfil it if he applies himself the right way. A scorer of two hat-tricks at under-20 level last season, his good work rate and team play impressed the Light Blues coaching staff. Stoney didn't play any senior games in 2013/14 but did make his competitive debut the previous campaign as a substitute against Clyde at Ibrox.

DAVID **TEMPLETON** LEE **WALLACE** TOM **WALSH**

	David Templeton	Lee Wallace	Tom Walsh
Position:	Midfielder	Defender	Midfielder
Date of Birth:	January 7, 1989	August 1, 1987	July 11, 1996
Nationality:	Scottish	Scottish	Scottish
Debut:	September 2, 2012 v Elgin City (H)	July 26, 2011 v Malmo (H)	December 8, 2012 v Stirling Albion (H)
Previous Club:	Heart of Midlothian	Heart of Midlothian	None

A tricky winger who stretches and torments his opponents, Templeton can open up rivals and create chances both for himself and others. Often a scorer of spectacular long-range goals, the ex-Hearts player has had fitness problems at times during his stay at Ibrox but shown how valuable he can be when he has been in the side. He debuted for Rangers in September 2012 against Elgin just three days after netting for the Jambos against Liverpool at Anfield.

Arguably the star man in Ally McCoist's squad, vice-captain Wallace is one of the team's biggest attacking threats despite usually playing at left-back. After playing understudy to Saša Papac, the Scotland international has made that spot his own now and was the club's Player of the Year and Players' Player of the Year in 2014. He has also won the PFA Scotland Division Three and League One Player of the Year prizes in the last two seasons.

A promising youngster who can play out wide or in a more central midfield role, Scotland youth cap Walsh came on as a substitute at just 16 years old against Stirling Albion in December 2012 but injuries since then have limited his progress. Armed with an abundance of talent, 2014/15 is a big campaign for the Kilmarnock kid as he looks to put his fitness issues behind him and push back into the senior side once again.

Ibrox Arrivals

Once again it was a busy summer transfer window for Rangers as they continued to rebuild the squad in order to push for promotion back to the top flight.

Here's a look at the new faces recruited by the Light Blues in the aftermath of the successful 2013/14 campaign.

KENNY MILLER

Position: Striker
Date of Birth: December 23, 1979
Nationality: Scottish
Previous Club: Vancouver Whitecaps

Not many players get the chance to play for Rangers three times but Miller falls into that category having come back to the club in June. He also put pen to paper on deals at Ibrox in

2000 and 2008 and his second spell at Gers was more successful than his first. Among his highlights were a winner in the 2010 League Cup final, when St Mirren were beaten by a single goal late on despite playing against just nine men. Miller's best campaign in Glasgow was undoubtedly the 2010/11 term, when he had scored 22 times by January. With his contract close to ending, he was sold to Bursaspor but is back at the club he grew up supporting once again.

DARREN McGREGOR

Position: Defender
Date of Birth: August 7, 1985
Nationality: Scottish
Previous Club: St Mirren

McGregor was a surprise signing in many people's eyes when he came to Ibrox in June but he's a player admired by the club for some time after a string of steady displays for former side St Mirren. The defender has had knee problems in the past but turned out 38 times for the Buddies in 2013/14 so came to Gers in excellent condition. Having started his career at Cowdenbeath, McGregor had two spells with them and helped them to the Third Division title in 2006. He has also experienced junior football with Arniston Rangers but has plenty of top-flight football behind him as well following four years in Paisley. While not a regular scorer, McGregor is versatile and can play centrally or on the right.

KRIS BOYD

Position: Striker
Date of Birth: August 18, 1983
Nationality: Scottish
Previous Club: Kilmarnock

A scorer 128 times in all competitions for Rangers in his first spell at the club, Boyd is one of only 17 men to have hit a century of league goals for the Light Blues in their 142-year history. The highest scorer in SPL history, he came back to Ibrox after an excellent campaign with Kilmarnock, where

his 22 strikes almost single-handedly kept them in the Premiership last term. Boyd's winner at Hibernian on the final day of the regular season ensured survival and his good form earned him a recall to the Scotland squad. The striker has also played south of the border with Middlesbrough and Nottingham Forest, Turkish side Eskişehirspor and turned out in the MLS alongside fellow Rangers player Stevie Smith for Portland Timbers.

MARIUS ŽALIŪKAS

Position: Defender
Date of Birth: November 10, 1983
Nationality: Lithuanian
Previous Club: Leeds United

Žaliūkas is a player Rangers have had an interest in for some time and he joined the club in July after spending time on trial at Murray Park in September 2013. A player with vast experience of Scottish football after seven years at Hearts – during which he was the club captain at Tynecastle for a spell – the Lithuanian is another person who has good knowledge of the game in this country. Most recently at Leeds United, Žaliūkas – a Scottish Cup winner with the Jambos in 2012 – spent just under a year at Elland Road and is expected to bring a physical game to the Light Blues' defence when he plays. He is familiar with the likes of Lee Wallace and Ian Black having played alongside them in Edinburgh.

LEE ROBINSON

Position: Goalkeeper
Date of Birth: July 2, 1986
Nationality: English
Previous Club: Raith Rovers

Goalkeeper Robinson signed a season-long deal with Rangers in August after regular number one Cammy Bell hurt his shoulder in a league match against Falkirk. He consequently became the third player to return to the club over the summer having been there previously as a teenager. Robinson only played 12 minutes for the team in his first stint at Ibrox as a substitute for Ronald Waterreus in a 2-0 win over Hearts in May 2006. Born south of the border in Sunderland, he has been at a number of clubs at home and abroad since then and won the Challenge Cup in each of the last two seasons with Queen of the South then Raith Rovers, beating Gers 1-0 with the Fifers at Easter Road.

BORN IN THE USA!

Rangers warmed up for 2014/15 with an extensive pre-season programme that saw them play nine games in four countries and cover more than 15,000 miles in the process!

They began with two matches against Highland League sides Buckie Thistle and Brora as they spent five days at a training camp in Sutherland.

In among the hard work done there, Ally McCoist, Kenny McDowall and Ian Durrant took time away from training to meet some local armed forces members.

It was a good trip and as fitness rose in the group, a 3-0 win against the Jags was recorded before a 1-1 draw at Dudgeon Park in the other fixture.

From there, the squad returned to Glasgow briefly and beat Fulham 4-2 behind closed doors before setting off on a North American tour.

First up were two games in the USA and before the first one – a 3-1 loss to Ventura County Fusion - ex-Gers captain Carlos Bocanegra popped by to say hello.

The team also took a dip in the Pacific Ocean before moving on to Sacramento, where players met fans at an exclusive signing session for NARSA members.

That was before a 2-1 win was recorded against Sacramento Republic and it was the same outcome in the first of two friendlies in Canada against Victoria Highlanders.

The match in British Columbia started spectacularly as skydivers dropped into Centennial Stadium to drop the match ball off!

Rangers rounded off their stay across the Atlantic with a 1-0 success against Ottawa Fury at their impressive new TD Place home.

And after another closed-doors victory against Partick courtesy of Lewis Macleod's goal, there was a 2-0 defeat to Derby in front of around 10,000 away fans at the iPro Stadium.

Youth Review

Danny Stone

Gordon Durie

The 2013/14 season wasn't just a successful one at senior level for Rangers, with the club's under-20s also prospering in a memorable campaign.

Under new coaches Gordon Durie, Billy Kirkwood and Jim Sinclair, a relatively young squad of players competed extremely well and landed silverware in the form of the SFA Youth Cup.

Gers went into the campaign having claimed the SFL Reserve League the previous term ahead of closest challengers Morton and Queen's Park.

Given it was won using a pool largely comprised of teenage prospects, hopes were high of another good year in the new SPFL age group competition.

The Light Blues were one of 16 teams in a new league created as a result of the merger of the SPL and SFL.

Along with each of the 12 top-flight sides, Durie's side competed alongside Falkirk, Dunfermline and Hamilton.

There was an allowance for over-aged players to take part as well and that meant Ally McCoist's fringe players could get valuable game time too.

The season began well and following a 0-0 draw with Hamilton in Airdrie, three victories in a row took the side to the top of the table.

Darren Ramsay

A thrilling 5-4 triumph against Dunfermline was the first of those as Rangers played their opening home match at Dumbarton.

The Sons' Bet Butler Stadium

Greg Pascazio

outstanding as they went 19 games unbeaten in all competitions in a run stretching more than five months.

After a three-week break initially, a 6-0 Youth Cup win over Dumbarton at Auchenhowie in which Danny Stoney scored the first of two hat-tricks in nine days set a good tone.

Three days later, a spirited comeback saw the swifts come from behind to draw 2-2 at Dundee United and they followed that result up with a 5-0 thrashing of Falkirk.

Two more 2-2 draws with Inverness and St Johnstone – in which the team again trailed twice each time – demonstrated great character.

And with belief rising, five successive victories including one in the Cup ensured 2013 ended on the right note.

The knockout competition win was emphatic as Hibs, one of the sides challenging for the league, were comprehensively beaten 5-1.

was to become a familiar scene for Durie's kids as they hosted games there, at Ibrox and at the club's Murray Park training complex.

But it was two more away outings which took the team to the summit, a 3-2 victory against Ross County in Inverness and a narrow 2-1 win at St Mirren.

Although Gers had started well in terms of results, Durie wasn't altogether happy with the way his youngsters were performing.

And a combination of losses to Aberdeen and Motherwell and the cancellation of fixtures because of international call-ups saw the Light Blues drop into the bottom half of the table.

It ended up being a turning point for Rangers and their response was

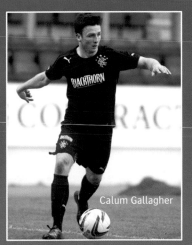
Calum Gallagher

A 3-0 victory at Partick was marred by Kyle Hutton's leg break on an otherwise good night at Firhill.

And although Dean Shiels was sent off early against Kilmarnock, Tom Walsh and Calum Gallagher's strikes still secured a positive outcome.

Stoney's winner against Hamilton was crucial as Gers again had to play with 10 men following Greg Pascazio's dismissal.

And Andy Murdoch and Calum Gallagher found the net at Dunfermline to send the squad into its winter break in good spirits.

With a month off over the festive period into January, the pause in play arguably came at a bad time for Durie's team.

Tom Walsh

Luca Gasparotto

A 1-1 draw with Hearts was a minor setback ahead of wins against Dundee United – with Craig Halkett grabbing the only goal – and Inverness in the Highlands.

Drawing 0-0 then did more for the Light Blues than it did for the Hibees, who were starting to run out of games to keep themselves ahead of Glasgow's big two.
A second 2-2 draw with St Johnstone was frustrating after Rangers had cruised to a two-goal lead before the break.

But the side made up for that with another five victories which set up a final-day decider against Celtic.

But if the coach had any fears about his players not picking up from where they left off, they were quickly shattered when the action resumed.

Four more league successes against Ross County, Hibs, St Mirren and Aberdeen – with just one goal lost in the process – took the team up the table.

And a 10th win in a row in all competitions against Dunfermline took the under-20s into the last four of the SFA Youth Cup.

Gers were slowly getting their extra games played and a three-horse race to the title was developing between themselves, city rivals Celtic and Hibs.

There were a couple of gritty victories in that haul, including a 2-1 success at Kilmarnock which saw auxiliary striker Halkett score moments after coming on as a substitute.

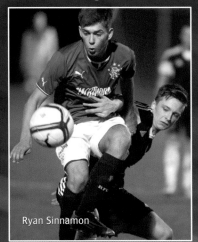
Ryan Sinnamon

His performance then ensured he played up front against a weakened Hearts team and

Dylan Dykes scores a penalty in a 2-1 win over Inverness in March

Kristian Gibson rides a tackle as Rangers draw 0-0 away to Hibernian

two more goals helped his side to a 4-1 win over them in Newtongrange.

A 2-1 win against Motherwell at Fir Park was monumental too and despite Chris Hegarty's sending off, Ryan Sinnamon fired home a late winner after Calum Gallagher's opener.

With a 4-0 thrashing of Falkirk at Westfield, Rangers knew avoiding defeat in their last match against Celtic would give them the title.
As it was, the derbies against the Parkhead side proved decisive and 2-0 victories for the east end outfit at home and away gave them the crown.

Nevertheless, Durie's kids had impressed and given all but one of their regulars are still

Jamie Burrows

eligible to play as under-20s this season, they perhaps even exceeded expectations. Despite missing out on the title by just one point, there was still a chance for Gers to finish with a trophy.

They had beaten St Mirren 1-0 in the semi-finals of the SFA Youth Cup in Paisley to progress to the deciding match at the same venue.

Andy Murdoch

Darren Ramsay's stunning extra-time goal had been enough to separate the sides and set up a meeting with Hearts.

Although the Jambos had finished the campaign six points adrift at the foot of the table, they were favourites to come out on top.

The reason for that was the fact several of their best youngsters had been playing regular first-team football rather than in the SPFL Under-20 League.

Rangers celebrate winning the SFA Youth Cup on penalties against Hearts

Much like their season had done, Rangers got stronger the longer the game went on and they had chances to win but couldn't take them and penalties were required.

What followed was one of the most dramatic shoot-outs the club has ever been involved in at any level.

Every outfield player still on the park ended up taking a kick, with the score locked at 7-7 after 10 penalties each. That meant the goalkeepers had to take their turn and having saved three times already, Gers' Liam Kelly scored his then stopped a fourth to give his team the glory.

It was a sensational triumph and one which was richly deserved for a team which gelled and grew as one over the course of a thrilling campaign.

Durie said: "I was delighted for the boys. They had the disappointment of missing out on the league but they showed great character to win the cup instead.

And when the teams lined up before kick-off, the Edinburgh side had 160 senior appearances for the season in their first XI compared with only seven in the Gers team.

It was to be expected that Hearts would have the better of the contest at times and they went in front through Sam Nicholson.

But Pascazio equalised and although Billy King put the team ahead once immediately, header forced Tynecastle again almost Halkett's late extra time.

Liam Kelly scores what turned out to be the winner against the Jambos

Keeper Kelly made four saves in the shoot-out success including this effort

"They were up for the game and while I don't think they played too well in the first half, our substitutes helped us get back into it.

"I've got to say the boys were fantastic all season. They worked really hard and they got their rewards in the end.

"You get what you deserve in football and even if we'd lost to Hearts, I would still have been proud of the players.

Craig Halkett celebrates his late goal which forced extra-time

"I think they deserved to win though and to pick up a bit of silverware at the end of the season was just fantastic."

A **Centre** of **Excellence**

Rangers fans are used to seeing their team playing at a packed-out Ibrox Stadium but it's at their Murray Park training centre where they work on a day-to-day basis each week.

Opened in July 2001 at a cost of £14 million, it was the vision of former Light Blues manager Dick Advocaat.

When he arrived in Glasgow as a replacement for Walter Smith three years earlier, Gers trained at several public venues around Glasgow.

Advocaat couldn't believe that was the case at a club of such high standing and he helped engineer a move to what remains one of the top facilities of its kind in European football.

Murray Park's main purpose is to serve as a first-team base but it's also where Rangers' youth academy players learn their trade.

And the centre is designed in such a way that the teenagers working on one side of the building naturally aspire and push themselves to earn a place round on the senior wing.

The facilities available to Gers' youngsters are good but they're simple in comparison to those the first-team pool has at its disposal.

While emerging talents change in relatively plain, functional dressing rooms, Ally McCoist's

star players use something similar to what you'd find at a luxury health club.

There's a sauna, steam room, whirlpool and a hydrotherapy pool which is where recovery sessions in the days after matches will often take place.

It can also be used to assist players who are coming back from long-term injuries and the floor is adjustable to suit different needs.

The gym at Murray Park is crammed with top-of-the-range equipment so that the Light Blues have every chance of staying ahead of their rivals.

And a half-size indoor pitch allows everyone to continue training even when the weather is bad outside.

Located on Auchenhowie Road in Milngavie just outside Glasgow, the complex has played a key role in convincing many players to join the 54-time Scottish champions over the years.

It continues to be a fantastic asset for the club and is one which will help McCoist's men in their quest to get back to the Premiership.

Murray Park by Numbers

27 – A staggering 27 miles of hot water piping make up the undersoil heating system which protects the main professional pitch, something which cost £150,000 to install.

30 – The depth in feet of a lagoon behind the professional wing of the main building which recycles water for pitch drainage. It holds 1.7million gallons in all.

38 – The number of acres the entire site, with its six full-size and two-half size parks, a practice area, one indoor pitch and other training facilities, changing rooms and rehabilitation rooms, covers.

60 – Murray Park's indoor synthetic pitch is 60 metres long and 40 metres wide. Its surface closely mimics grass and is laid on a bed of rubber crumbs which provide cushioning and help to prevent injuries.

700 – On average, that's how many kits are washed every week in the £25,000 laundry room at Murray Park, with staff ensuring training gear and matchday strips are always prepared.

9,600 – This is the capacity in gallons of the complex's state-of-the-art hydrotherapy pool, which has a movable floor that can be adjusted in depth from just a few centimetres to 1.75 metres.

50,000 – Rangers' £50,000 video editing suite is linked to a remote-controlled camera on the professional pitch, which films every training session and allows the manager to request specific things are recorded. Footage can later be analysed in team meetings.

150,000 – The cost in pounds of equipment in the gym at Murray Park, where every machine is linked to the medical centre's computer system to allow players to be monitored.

LEE McCULLOCH'S DREAM TEAM

Lee McCulloch moved to Rangers in the summer of 2007 and he's experienced so many highs in his time with the club.

A three-time SPL winner, he has also claimed a trio of League Cups and enjoyed two Scottish Cup final victories with the Light Blues.

He played in the UEFA Cup final against Zenit St Petersburg too in 2008 and, more recently, has captained the team to the Third Division and League One titles.

Here the Ibrox skipper picks his favourite team of players who have turned out for the 54-times national champions.

GOALKEEPER: ALLAN MCGREGOR

"Allan's a massive Rangers fan and he welcomed me as soon as I came to the club. He's an

unbelievable goalkeeper and one of the best I've played with in my career.

"The boys used to call him the Mad Monk after a character in Mean Machine because of the way he comes to claim the ball and he's a great guy to have around the dressing room."

RIGHT-BACK: ALAN HUTTON

"I think Alan struggled a little bit in the early part of his career but Walter Smith coming back

to Rangers gave him the confidence to believe in himself.

"He got up and down the right side all day putting in good crosses and defended really well too. He's a big character and a fantastic player.

CENTRE-HALF: DAVID WEIR

"It's a no-brainer having David in my team. He was the captain at Rangers in the latter stages of his time at the club and he was an all-round leader of men.

"As well as being a fantastic player, he is a fantastic guy too and he has often been a shoulder to cry on for me."

CENTRE-HALF: RICHARD GOUGH

"Richard is a legend at the club and we've been lucky enough to train with him a good few

times when he has been back visiting Glasgow.

"He's always willing to help the young boys and he has all the same qualities as David in that respect. He's a massive influence."

LEFT-BACK: LEE WALLACE

"Lee is a really, really good player who could go on to perform at the very highest level one day if he wanted to.

"He has shown great commitment to Rangers and feels he can reach the top again with us by helping the team back into the Champions League once more."

RIGHT-MIDFIELD: STEVEN DAVIS

"Davo had a great career with Rangers and that was reflected by the fact he captained the team. He is also Northern Ireland's captain as well.

He has phenomenal ability and pace and he scored some really good, important goals for the team during his time at Ibrox."

CENTRAL-MIDFIELD: PAUL GASCOIGNE

"Gazza was a big-time player who delivered when it mattered so often. His hat-trick to win the league against Aberdeen in 1996 is a great example of that.

"I get emotional watching that. Another goal which stands out is his strike against Celtic at their place where he dinked it over the keeper and celebrated with the fans."

CENTRAL-MIDFIELD: BARRY FERGUSON

"Barry was the captain of the club when I came to Rangers and he was a tough player to play with if you were a new signing. I mean that in a good way.

"He'd give you a hard time but he'd do it to get the best out of you because 50,000 fans demand and expect high standards which he delivered."

LEFT-MIDFIELD: BRIAN LAUDRUP

"Laudrup's ability when he played, with the pace and standard of finishing he had, was brilliant to watch.

"I was lucky enough to play against him a few years ago in

pre-season when he turned out for Clyde and he still had it all even then in his late 30s."

STRIKER: KRIS BOYD

"Kris loves getting goals and he loves the club, as does his family. He's a player Rangers fans know all about and who they admire.

"The five he scored in one night against Dundee United to break the SPL scoring record spring to mind when I think about him and he's so ruthless in the penalty area."

STRIKER: ALLY McCOIST

"Alistair keeps telling me how many goals he scored for Rangers but he could talk me through every single one and tell me how good it was too.

"He was an amazing talent and any time he has joined in at training, he has called himself the gas man because when he comes on he turns the temperature up a few notches!"

Quiz

Think you know everything about Rangers? Let's see how you get on with our 20 questions on the Light Blues!

Don't worry if you're struggling because each question is based on information you'll find elsewhere in this book. Just do your research and you'll be a champion like the Ibrox side!

2013/14 Season

1. Which player scored the opening goal of the League One campaign in a 4-1 victory against Brechin City at Ibrox in August 2013?

2. How many hat-tricks did Lee McCulloch score last season and against which teams did he score them?

3. Which side did Honduran midfielder Arnold Peralta score his only competitive goal of 2013/14 against?

4. What was Rangers' best winning scoreline last season, a result which gave them their greatest league win since 1967?

5. Who grabbed four goals for Rangers against Forfar Athletic in December 2013 on the night of his mum Liz's birthday?

The Squad

1. How old was Tom Walsh when he made his senior Rangers debut against Stirling Albion in December 2012?

2. Light Blues winger Fraser Aird has represented Scotland at youth level but in which country was he born and raised?

3. Which English Premier League side did Gers' Tunisian defender Bilel Mohsni once have a trial with?

4. Which final position did Sébastien Faure help France to at the 2011 FIFA Under-20 World Cup in Columbia?

5. How many goals did Nicky Clark score in his final season with Queen of the South before he joined Rangers?

The Club

1. What is the current capacity of Ibrox Stadium?

2. How many times, including their win in 1972, have Rangers competed in the final of the European Cup Winners' Cup?

3. Which former Rangers manager was behind the building of and the move to the club's training ground at Murray Park in 2001?

4. True or false: Rangers once played at an area in Glasgow called Burnbank before they moved to Ibrox?

5. On which street is Rangers' Murray Park training centre located?

Miscellaneous

1. Not including as part of the Scottish national team, how many times did Sandy Jardine win the Scottish Football Writers' Player of the Year award?

2. Which team did Gordon Durie's Rangers under-20 side beat to win the SFA Youth Cup in 2013/14?

3. Who was the first new player to agree to join Rangers ahead of the start of the 2014/15 season?

4. Which Rangers player is the current holder of the Sam English Bowl for being the club's leading league scorer in the 2013/14 season?

5. Against which Highland League team did Rangers start their pre-season campaign in July 2014?

How did you score?

16-20 – Promotion to the Premiership!
11-15 – The play-offs beckon
6-10 – Another Championship year awaits
0-5 – Losers go back to League One

ANSWERS ON P60

Can you find the surnames of 20 Rangers Hall of Fame legends?
Words can go horizontally, vertically and diagonally in all eight directions.

```
L  R  K  M  J  F  M  A  R  O  G  X  R  Z  K
L  M  K  L  G  L  N  Y  J  V  N  F  T  V  E
E  N  Z  G  O  Z  I  D  P  E  H  R  P  K  C
D  T  V  I  W  S  T  A  S  H  E  W  L  D  N
D  O  T  E  N  K  J  K  H  B  P  G  Q  U  A
A  S  D  R  L  C  C  F  L  P  A  T  H  R  L
W  U  T  G  L  I  O  A  K  S  C  M  J  R  L
K  R  T  H  R  G  R  O  C  K  C  M  Y  A  A
L  O  O  F  G  K  N  O  P  C  Z  E  W  N  V
A  M  V  L  T  U  I  L  A  E  L  N  R  T  M
U  A  O  Z  Q  G  O  L  D  E  R  Y  N  Q  R
D  V  N  T  N  C  L  G  T  J  T  G  N  W  F
R  N  X  E  J  R  K  A  Q  W  B  R  A  N  D
U  L  K  F  J  D  H  C  J  A  R  D  I  N  E
P  T  M  M  H  C  O  L  L  U  C  C  M  Y  W
```

Albertz	Gascoigne	Jardine	McPhail
Amoruso	Goram	Klos	Novo
Brand	Gough	Laudrup	Ricksen
Cooper	Greig	McCall	Vallance
Durrant	Hateley	McCulloch	Waddell

ANSWERS ON P60

Eat like a Player

When you're a professional footballer, it's important to conduct yourself properly to stay ahead of your rivals and that means training and resting at the right times.

What you eat is really important too and a player has a much better chance of succeeding if he maintains a healthy, balanced diet.

Chef Paul Lafferty first started working with Rangers in 1990 and he cooks for the Light Blues players every day at their Murray Park training base as well as on matchdays.

He works closely with the club's coaches, sports scientists and medical staff to ensure Gers stars get all the nutrients they need to stay fit and strong.

Here Paul explains how to make one of the squad's favourite dishes, chorizo pasta with mixed vegetables.

Ingredients (for four people)

225g chorizo
½ red pepper
½ yellow pepper
½ green pepper
300g cherry tomatoes
1 red onion
1 courgette
2 garlic cloves
8-10 button mushrooms
2 tbsp olive oil
50ml vegetable stock
Sea salt and freshly ground black pepper
300-400g dried pasta, such as fusilli, conchiglie or penne
1 tsp mixed herbs
1 tsp dried chilli flakes

Preparation method

1 Boil a full kettle of water and prepare the vegetables. Dice each of the peppers and the red onion, quarter the mushrooms, slice the courgette and finely chop the garlic. Also slice the chorizo into bite-sized pieces. Preparation should take roughly 10 minutes.

2 Once the kettle is boiled, add 50ml of water to half a vegetable stock cube and mix. Add your pasta to the rest of the water and cook to packet instructions (8-10 minutes).

3 Heat the olive oil over a medium to high heat in a large wok and add the chorizo, frying for around a minute.

4 Add the peppers, red onion, courgette, cherry tomatoes and mushrooms and sauté for a further two minutes before adding the mixed herbs and chilli flakes.

5 Add vegetable stock to the wok to give the dish more moisture along with the chopped garlic cloves. Cook until the pasta is ready, lowering the heat if necessary, then add the drained pasta to the wok and mix.

6 Add another drizzle of olive oil and season to taste with salt and pepper. Serve with parmesan cheese, garlic bread and salad.

Why is this dish good for you?

"It has lots of different coloured vegetables and that is more important than you might think. They offer a lot of nutrition and different minerals and thanks to the fact there is four times more vitamin C in peppers compared with oranges, they have plenty of that too. There is no such thing as an unhealthy bit of food but you can keep an unhealthy diet if you eat lots of the same thing all the time and that can be counter-productive so this gives you a variety of stuff you should be eating on a day to day basis. There are green vegetables included which are always good as they produce energy and support the body's

immune system while cherry tomatoes fight against the stresses of exercise. People might not think much of the fact there are herbs in the recipe but they play a role too from the point of view they do things which help your body fight against diseases and illness. The dish includes meat, pasta and vegetables so you've got all the things which can help you keep a balanced diet."

When should you eat it?

"This is a great meal to have during pre-season because of how versatile it is. It's a really good recovery meal so you might have it for lunch or dinner after a heavy session of running as you are trying to get fit ahead of a new campaign. By the same token, there are obviously carbohydrates in the pasta so it could be had before you go out to work instead. You don't need to worry if you're not a fan of chorizo as that could be exchanged for any other continental meat such as

chicken. In that instance, I'd recommend cutting the chicken in a similar fashion and cooking it first before taking it out of the wok again and re-introducing towards the end along with the stock. That way you can poach it rather than overdo it. Whatever meat you include, it's a good thing to have because it helps build muscular strength and power and is full of protein."

What do the players think of it?

"This is probably one of the most popular dishes we make for the squad at Murray Park. There are quite a few players who will tell you this is their favourite and everyone in the group will ask for it at some time or another. If I was to ask my wife which meal she'd have as her last, she'd probably say this one – although I'd probably have to stick a bit more chorizo in! In the first week of pre-season, it is always one of the first dishes we have on for the players to eat in between sessions if they are training twice in one day."

The Treble Winners

Rangers have won the domestic Treble of the league, the Scottish Cup and the League Cup on seven different occasions – more than any other side in Scotland.

Six men have managed the team to those successes and here's a look at what each of them achieved in their time in charge.

BILL STRUTH
(1948/49)

Struth, a strict disciplinarian who was well known for his trademark doubled-breasted suits, is the most successful Rangers manager of all time and his achievements are reflected by the fact the Main Stand at Ibrox is now named after him. Of the 30 major honours he won, just three of them were grouped together in a single Treble. Given Struth was in charge for 34 years until 1954 and the League Cup only began in 1946, the chances are he'd have claimed more trios of trophies if he'd had more opportunities. The successes Gers enjoyed in 1948/49 saw them beat Raith 2-0 in the League Cup final, defeat Clyde 4-1 to collect the Scottish Cup and win the title by a point from Dundee in their last match.

SCOT SYMON
(1963/64)

Scot Symon shakes hands with Tottenham Hotspur manager Bill Nicholson

Symon, who went by a shortened version of his middle name Scotland, replaced Struth at the helm and was another success as he won 17 trophies, took Rangers to two European Cup Winners' Cup finals and oversaw the development of star players such as John Greig, Jim Baxter and Ronnie McKinnon. Having already played for the club, with the bulk of his appearances coming during World War II, the Treble victory of 1964 was among his finest. In a golden era at Ibrox, the League Cup came first that season as Jim Forrest's four goals inspired a 5-0 thrashing of Morton at Hampden Park in the deciding game. A six-point win in Division One was comfortable and Dundee lost 3-1 to the Light Blues in the competition climax of the Scottish Cup.

JOCK WALLACE
(1975/76 and 1977/78)

The only man to manage Rangers to two Trebles, Wallace also had two spells as boss and both of the clean sweeps came in his first. A hard taskmaster, he famously had the players running up and down the sand dunes in Gullane during pre-season. His unconventional methods clearly worked as Gers, having ended Celtic's dominance of the league a year earlier, won everything on offer in 1976. They beat their city rivals to the league crown by six points and defeated them 1-0 in the League Cup final, with Alex MacDonald scoring. Hearts then lost 3-1 in the Scottish Cup final, with Derek Johnstone getting the opener after 42 seconds and before the allotted 3pm kick-off time. Two years on, another Treble was clinched but Wallace left his position just a few days after a 2-1 Scottish Cup triumph against Aberdeen.

he had inherited from Smith and thrust it to the top of the pile on all fronts within Scotland again. In particular, Rod Wallace and Jörg Albertz's goals were crucial in a league campaign which resulted in the title being won at Celtic Park after an emphatic 3-0 victory. That came after a 2-1 defeat of St Johnstone at the same venue to claim the League Cup and a single-goal victory against Celtic – with Wallace scoring again – made it a dream first season for Advocaat as the Scottish Cup was secured.

Jock Wallace and Walter Smith

WALTER SMITH
(1992/93)

Smith's men came within a whisker of the first ever Champions League final in 1993 but claiming a domestic Treble and going 44 games unbeaten certainly went some way to making up for not going further abroad. With Ally McCoist firing himself to a second consecutive European Golden Boot, he and Mark Hateley's goals proved to be so crucial that year as they found the net 78 times between them. Even though two points were awarded for a win then rather than three, Rangers were utterly dominant as they won the league by nine points to claim their fifth of nine in a row. Smith oversaw a pair of 2-1 wins over Aberdeen to claim the League Cup and the Scottish Cup too as a first clean sweep in 15 years was achieved.

ALEX McLEISH
(2002/03)

McLeish had a lot to prove to Rangers fans when he arrived at Ibrox from Hibernian without having won a major trophy but he would go on to collect seven of them at Ibrox including each of the domestic prizes in 2002/03. Having beaten Celtic in the final of the Scottish Cup the previous campaign, his side did the same again in the League Cup as Claudio Caniggia

DICK ADVOCAAT
(1998/99)

Dutchman Advocaat had a lot of work to do when he was appointed as Smith's successor in 1998 but he invested well in the transfer market and brought in a number of prominent players from Europe to rebuild the ageing squad and Peter Løvenkrands' goals sealed a 2-1 win. The league was claimed in dramatic circumstances on the final day as the Light Blues stayed ahead of Celtic in the table by a single goal as their 6-1 rout of Dunfermline bettered the Parkhead outfit's 4-0 win at Kilmarnock. In his final appearance for the club, Lorenzo Amoruso got the only goal to give Gers a 1-0 victory over Dundee in the Scottish Cup to complete the set of trophies.

Remember When?

This season Rangers are bidding to get back into the top flight of Scottish football, where they have won a world record total of 54 league titles.

During their days among the elite they won many other major honours and here's a look back at five games from recent years which led to trophy success.

Dundee United 0-3 Rangers
SPL, Tannadice
May 25, 2009

Rangers were looking to win their first SPL title since their dramatic last-day success in 2005 known as Helicopter Sunday after two late goals for Motherwell saw them beat Celtic and send the Light Blues to the top of the table in the last seconds of the campaign. Four years on from that, the championship again went down to the final 90 minutes and Gers had the advantage as they sat two points clear of their Old Firm rivals. They knew a draw probably wouldn't be enough to secure the trophy though as Celtic had a better goal difference and Walter Smith's team started positively as they went ahead through Kyle Lafferty after just six minutes. Pedro Mendes added a second just before half-time and Kris Boyd made sure with the third. In the end, Celtic could only draw at home with Hearts and Rangers came out on top by four points.

Rangers 1-0 Celtic
SPL, Ibrox
February 28, 2010

This match didn't actually secure the league title but the result all but ended the title race as a contest. Rangers had been much stronger than Celtic in the first months of the SPL and were seven points ahead of them going into this game. A draw would have suited the Light Blues far more than their rivals but the Ibrox team was determined to win and deliver another blow to the Parkhead outfit's aspirations. Substitute Maurice Edu had the ball in the net with his first touch but his strike was disallowed and the longer the game went on without a breakthrough, the more frustrating it became for Gers. It seemed Celtic would just cling on to their title hopes but Edu forced home in a goalmouth scramble nearly three minutes into injury time to grab a stunning late victory. With a 10-point lead, Rangers went from strength to strength and secured a second successive crown with a 1-0 win at Hibernian on April 25.

St Mirren 0-1 Rangers
Scottish League Cup Final, Hampden Park
March 21, 2010

Rangers were favourites to come out on top in this match after winning four of their previous five meetings with St Mirren in 2009/10 and drawing the other but they faced an uphill task when they had two men sent off in the second half. Kevin Thomson was first to go for a reckless lunge and young defender Danny Wilson soon followed for preventing a goalscoring opportunity just outside the penalty area. With just nine players on the park for the final 19 minutes, Gers were on the ropes and the Saints grew in confidence but then something remarkable happened as Kenny Miller put the Ibrox outfit in front against the odds. David Weir broke forward and spread the ball wide to Steven Naismith, whose cross was diverted into the net with a glancing header by Miller. It was a real demonstration of hunger and desire from the Light Blues, with Walter Smith orchestrating things ever so well from the touchline.

Rangers 2-1 Celtic
Scottish League Cup Final, Hampden Park
March 20, 2011

Rangers were the better side in the regulation 90 minutes against Glasgow rivals Celtic in the 2011 League Cup final but the sides were locked at 1-1 after the excellent Steven Davis' goal was cancelled out by Joe Ledley. Gers pushed on in extra time and eventually got their winner which was richly deserved. Nikica Jelavić got it with his first derby goal and it was an excellent strike on the break. Substitute Vladimír Weiss – who later revealed he was playing with a broken foot – took a quick free kick and that allowed Jelavić to break clear. Despite being pursued by two defenders, the Croatian stroked past Fraser Forster and saw the ball hit the inside of one post, roll across the line and into the netting on the other side of the goal. He wheeled away in celebration and little wonder as his effort ended up being what won the trophy for Rangers for the 27th time.

Kilmarnock 1-5 Rangers
SPL, Rugby Park
May 15, 2011

For the fifth time in eight years, Rangers and Celtic went into the final day of the 2010/11 SPL still in contention for the title. For the fourth time, it was the Light Blues who came out on top with one of their most pulsating victories of all time. They were ahead of the Parkhead outfit by a point going into the final fixtures and knew they had to simply match their Old Firm opponents' result against Motherwell to stay at the

summit. The way they did that was phenomenal as three goals in the opening seven minutes at Kilmarnock had away fans singing about Gers being champions with most of the game still to play. Kyle Lafferty broke the deadlock, Steven Naismith added a second and Lafferty struck again. Nikica Jelavić then added a fourth just after half-time and Lafferty completed his hat-trick to ensure Walter Smith, in his final match as Rangers manager, bowed out on a high with the title.

Quiz ANSWERS

2013/14 Season:

1 Chris Hegarty
2 Three against East Fife, Arbroath and Airdrieonians
3 Stranraer
4 8-0 (against Stenhousemuir)
5 Nicky Clark

The Squad:

1 16
2 Canada
3 West Ham
4 Fourth
5 41

The Club:

1 50,987
2 Three (1961, 1967 and 1972)
3 Dick Advocaat
4 True
5 Auchenhowie Road

Miscellaneous:

1 Two (In 1975 and 1986)
2 Hearts
3 Kenny Miller
4 Jon Daly
5 Buckie Thistle

Wordsearch ANSWERS

They SAID IT!

Words can carry so much meaning in football and particularly at Rangers, where so many prophetic things have been said over the last 142 years.

Here are some of the most memorable quotes from Light Blues players, coaches and staff from the past and present.

"My only regret was coming too late and leaving too early."
Mark Hateley

"I only support two teams; Rangers, and whoever is playing Celtic."
Davie Cooper

Jim Baxter

"The wives of Celtic fans used to send me letters thanking me for sending their husbands home early."
Jim Baxter

"To be a Ranger is to sense the sacred trust of upholding all that such a name means in this shrine of football."
Bill Struth

"I'm not bothered about where we play, I'm just happy to be playing for Rangers."
Lewis Macleod

"I never even went into the Blue Room at Ibrox until I had won every medal I could with Rangers."
John Brown

"The best year of my life was the last of my career. Playing for Rangers was my dream and it meant everything to my family."
Andy Gray

"Sorry, Mr Chairman, but this is the earliest I've been late in a long time."
Ally McCoist

"I hope to be here so long they have to kick me out!"
Andy Goram

"If I have one regret in my career, it is that I did not join Rangers a lot sooner."
Ray Wilkins

"This club grows in your heart and stays there forever."
Saša Papac

"My team don't play friendlies, they play challenge matches."
Jock Wallace

"Playing for a club like this is something you dream about when you are a kid at school."
Lee McCulloch

"Let the others come at us, we welcome the chase."
Bill Struth

"A wonderful club when you're winning, a tough old club when you're not."
Richard Gough

Andy Goram

Where's Broxi?

RANGERS mascot Broxi Bear joined Light Blues fans in the crowd at an away game against Ayr United last season but can you see where he's standing in this picture?